Reading for Every Child
Phonics

Grade 2

by
Linda Armstrong

Published by Instructional Fair
an imprint of
Frank Schaffer Publications®

Instructional Fair

Author: Linda Armstrong
Editor: Krista Fanning
Interior Designer: Lori Kibbey

Frank Schaffer Publications®

Instructional Fair is an imprint of Frank Schaffer Publications.

Send all inquiries to:
Frank Schaffer Publications
3195 Wilson Drive NW
Grand Rapids, Michigan 49534

Reading for Every Child: Phonics—grade 2
ISBN: 0-7424-2832-X

3 4 5 6 7 8 9 10 PAT 10 09 08 07

Table of Contents

Reading First 4
About This Book 5
Skills Assessment 6

Consonants
Reviewing Consonant Sounds 8
Ride the Rails 9
Down the Slide 10
Bathtub Fun! 11
Here's the Clue 12
What Was the Queen Doing? 13
Our Earth 14
Rhyming Riddles 15

Vowels
Reviewing Vowel Sounds 16
What's Missing? 17
My Dog and I 18
The Best Nest 19
Use the Side Gate 20
My Code 21
Up on the Hill 22
A Day Riddle 23

Digraphs
Whale of a Word 24
Scrambled! 25
Castles 26
Who Is Hiding in the Trees? 27
E or I? 28
Free Time 29
Stirring the Soup 30
A Sweet Treat 31
Beetlerella's Bug Ball 32
Inching Along 33

Blends
Stack and Spell 34
Fish School 35
A Slippery Puzzle 36
Crab Walk 37
Train Tracks 38
One Knight's Knots 39
Spring Flowers 40
A Trip to the Bank 41
The Old Tower 42

Diphthongs
Down for the Count 43
Ship Ahoy! 44
A Good Book 45
Shining at Night 46
Blast Off! 47

Compound Words
Compound Words 48
Everything, Except Onions 49
Play Ball! 50
Rays of Sunshine 51
Compound Critters 52
Compound Words Puzzle 53

Syllabication
Breaking It Down 54
Feel the Beat 55
Dividing Syllables 56
Chipmunk's Challenge 57

Affixes and Plurals
Taking a Walk 58
Wolfs or Wolves? 59
Adding Endings 60
A Bushel of Apples 61
One Sheep, Two Sheep 62
The Dog's Bone 63
Untidy Room 64

Contractions, Homophones, and Sight Words
You're a Winner! 65
I'll Call You Later 66
Two Peas in a Pod 67
Dear Deer 68
Missing Marks 69
Fill-It-In Puzzle 70
Morning ABCs 71
Eight on My Plate 72
Friends to the End 73
The Floating Hand 74

Cultivating a Love of Reading 75
Resources for Reading Teachers 76
Answer Key 77

Reading First

The Reading First program is part of the No Child Left Behind Act. This program is based on research by the National Reading Panel that identifies five key areas for early reading instruction—phonemic awareness, phonics, fluency, vocabulary, and comprehension.

Phonemic Awareness
Phonemic awareness focuses on a child's understanding of letter sounds and the ability to manipulate those sounds. Listening is a crucial component, as the emphasis at this level is on sounds that are heard and differentiated in each word the child hears.

Phonics
After students recognize sounds that make up words, they must then connect those sounds to *written* text. An important part of phonics instruction is systematic encounters with letters and letter combinations.

Fluency
Fluent readers are able to recognize words quickly. They are able to read aloud with expression and do not stumble over words. The goal of fluency is to read more smoothly and with *comprehension*.

Vocabulary
In order to understand what they read, students must first have a solid base of vocabulary words. As students increase their vocabulary knowledge, they also increase their comprehension and fluency.

Comprehension
Comprehension is "putting it all together" to understand what has been read. With both fiction and nonfiction texts, students become active readers as they learn to use specific comprehension strategies before, during, and after reading.

About This Book

Learning to read is a complex process involving many interrelated skills. Supporting current state standards, *Reading for Every Child: Phonics* is designed to help students develop the skills necessary to become independent readers.

Listening to the lively read alouds suggested in the activity sections will motivate second graders to seek out independent reading materials that suit their interests and abilities. They will build reading speed and confidence through enjoyable practice.

As they complete reproducible worksheets in this book, students will review alphabetical order as well as basic vowel and consonant sounds. Through puzzle solving, game playing, listening, writing, and sharing, they will expand their knowledge of consonant blends, special vowel sounds, irregular forms, and unusual spelling patterns.

While enjoying the activities in *Reading for Every Child: Phonics,* young readers will practice decoding longer, more complex words. They will become more proficient at using structural cues. They will become more familiar with compound words, syllables, prefixes, suffixes, plurals, and inflectional endings. They will also work with homophones, contractions, and singular possessives.

The exercises included here, along with verse collections available in the library or online, will give second graders more practice with rhymes and their cousins, the word families known as rimes. Reading different types of sentences aloud will give students practice with expressive reading.

Activities in this book showcase two hundred basic sight words in many different ways. Some are included as examples of consonant and vowel patterns. Others are featured in separate sentence-building exercises.

Reading for Every Child: Phonics provides a flexible set of tools to support your reading program. The worksheets and activities included here may be used in many ways. Feel free to skip around or modify them to meet your needs.

Skills Assessment

Consonant Blends and Digraphs

Directions: Circle the letters that complete each word.

1. 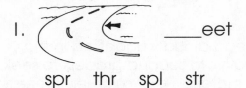 ___eet

    spr thr spl str

5. 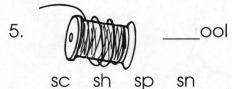 ___ool

    sc sh sp sn

2.  ___air

    qu ch wh fr

6.  ba___

    st nt nk sh

3. ___unk

    sl sk sp sn

7.  di___

    st nt nk sh

4.  ___aid

    tr th br cr

8.  ne___

    st nt nk sh

Vowel Digraphs, Diphthongs, and Other Vowel Sounds

Directions: Fill in the circle in front of the word that names each picture.

9. ○ bill
   ○ ball
   ○ bowl

12. ○ cuff
    ○ cow
    ○ cap

10. ○ paw
    ○ pat
    ○ paste

13. ○ broad
    ○ braid
    ○ bread

11. ○ late
    ○ lot
    ○ light

14. ○ book
    ○ beak
    ○ bake

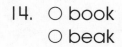

Skills Assessment (cont.)

Compound Words and Prefixes

Directions: Circle the word that names each picture.

15.

    suntan   sunset   sunburn

16.

    fireman   fireworks   fireplace

17.

    pinecone   chipmunk   toothpaste

18.

    birdhouse   firehouse   lighthouse

19.

    doorway   roadway   highway

20.

    undo   unhappy   unpaid

Inflectional Forms, Contractions, and Plurals

Directions: Read each sentence and the words under it. Write the word that makes sense on the line.

21. _____ my turn!

22. Is Jack _____ to the party?

23. There are ten _____ in line.

24. He _____ come with us.

25. I have two _____ in my desk.

26. She carried the two _____.

books
coming
won't
It's
dishes
children

Reviewing Consonant Sounds

Breaking It Down

Write a rime on the board and pass out consonant cards to the class. Invite students to blend their consonants with the rime and say the syllable. Point out that pieces of words, called syllables, are often not words by themselves. Then write the syllables *re*, *frig*, *er*, *a*, and *tor* on the board. Encourage volunteers to read each one. Write the word *refrigerator* without the spaces between and challenge the class to read it. On another day, repeat the process with a different polysyllabic word.

Consonant Shape Books

Find or create simple outline shapes for any of the following objects: ball, car, dog, fish, bunch of grapes, house, jewel, kite, leg, mail, nail, pail, rabbit, seal, tooth, umbrella, vase, world, yarn, or zipper. Encourage students to use your pattern to create a front and back construction-paper cover and several pages. Invite them to find words in magazines and books that contain the consonant. Encourage them to copy the words into the shape book. When the books are complete, allow time for students to meet in small groups to share what they have found.

Daffy-nitions

Invent a silly definition, such as "a crayon that falls on the floor." Encourage students to think of a nonsense word that could fit the definition, such as *crayoor*, or *fayon*. Write the nonsense word and the definition on a chart. Don't be surprised if your class starts to develop a playful private language. Other possible subjects for invented words include the first student to line up, the office monitor, a student who forgets lunch money, and a favorite book.

Song Lyrics Jive

Write the words of favorite songs on charts or overhead transparencies. Point to them as the class sings. Familiarity with the lyrics will help struggling students relate sounds they hear to letters on the page. To review target sounds, encourage the class to make up new, silly lyrics to favorite tunes. For example, to review the /t/ sound, the lyrics to "My Bonny Lies Over the Ocean" could become:

> My TV is covered with toothpaste. My tickets are covered with tea. A tiger has stolen my suitcase. Oh, bring back my tulips to me.

Other songs that are fun to reinvent include "Polly Wolly Doodle" and "On Top of Old Smoky."

Ride the Rails

Directions: Look at each picture. Read the words on the train. Write the word that matches the picture on each line.

1. _____nut_____

2. _____

3. _____

4. _____

5. _____

6. _____

7. _____

8. _____

9. _____

10. _____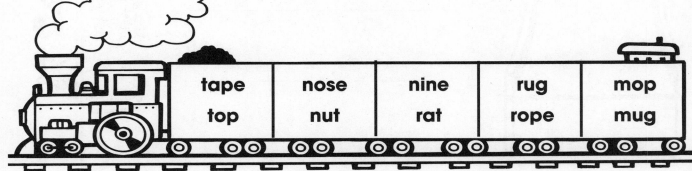

| tape | nose | nine | rug | mop |
| top | nut | rat | rope | mug |

0-7424-2832-X *Reading for Every Child: Phonics*

Phonics

Down the Slide

Directions: Look at each picture. Read the words on the slide. Write a word that begins with the same sound on the line. Use each word one time.

look

seal

cookie

desk

seven

cat

dime

sun

cow

leaf

1. _____ cat _____

2. _____

3. _____

4. _____

5. _____

6. _____

7. _____

8. _____

9. _____

10. _____

6

Published by Instructional Fair. Copyright protected.   0-7424-2832-X *Reading for Every Child: Phonics*

initial consonants (p, b, f, v)

Bathtub Fun!

Directions: Read each sentence. Write **p**, **b**, **f**, or **v** inside
the bubble to complete the word.

1. The dog chased the red (f)ox.

2. We had to take our cat to the ( )et.

3. You can cook eggs in a ( )an.

4. I wondered what was inside the big ( )ox.

5. She turned on the ( )an to cool down.

6. I put the ( )illow over my head.

7. The ( )ear came out of his den for food.

8. We can all drive to the store in her ( )an.

9. He was the tallest ( )oy in his class.

10. My little brother is ( )ive years old.

Phonics

Here's the Clue

Directions: For each line, read the first word and the clue. Change the first letter to **h**, **k**, or **w** to make a new word that fits the clue. Write the new word on the line.

Word	Clue	New Word
1. bat	Put it on your head.	*hat*
2. land	It can hold a pen.	_____
3. bite	You can fly it.	_____
4. bell	It has water in it.	_____
5. ball	It keeps things in or out.	_____
6. did	It is a baby goat.	_____
7. bug	Give it to your mom.	_____
8. bill	It is a high place.	_____
9. jam	You eat it with eggs.	_____
10. cave	You see it on the sea.	_____
11. pick	You do it with a foot.	_____
12. dome	It is where you live.	_____

Phonics

What Was the Queen Doing?

Directions: Find and circle the hidden words. The letters not circled will reveal a hidden message.

jam	quick
jar	quiet
jeans	quill
jelly	quit
job	quiz
jug	zebra
juice	zero
quack	zipper
queen	zoom

```
E  A  Q  U  I  E  T  Z  J  T  Q
J  A  M  Q  Q  I  N  E  E  G  U
Q  B  R  Z  U  U  E  R  A  Q  I
U  J  U  G  E  I  I  O  N  U  C
I  A  Z  D  A  B  Z  L  S  E  K
T  J  N  I  D  H  R  O  L  E  N
E  J  A  J  P  Y  M  A  Z  N  N
M  T  E  R  U  P  Q  U  O  R  N
K  R  T  L  B  I  E  M  J  O  B
Z  O  O  M  L  V  C  R  E  H  L
Q  U  A  C  K  Y  P  E  T  M  V
```

Now write the letters that are not circled on the lines below. Write them in order from left to right, row by row. They will tell you what the queen was doing while the king was busy in his counting house.

What was the queen doing?

___ ___ ___ ___ ___ ___ ___   ___ ___ ___ ___ ___

___ ___ ___ ___   ___ ___ ___ ___ ___ ___

This king and queen are from a famous rhyme. Can you name it?

Phonics

Our Earth

Directions: Read each sentence. Write one of the rocket's letters on the line to complete the word.

1. Earth is a plane _t_ .

2. It is the thir__ planet from the sun.

3. There are eigh__ other planets.

4. Some are big an__ some are small.

5. Some planets are very ho__.

6. Others are very col__.

7. Earth is jus__ right for life.

8. The su__ is really a star.

9. I__ is made of hot gas.

10. It sends hea__ to all of the planets.

11. Planets close to the su__ get the most heat.

12. Planets tha__ are far away do not get as much heat or light.

Rhyming Riddles

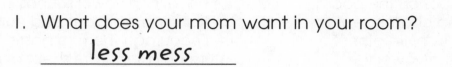

Directions: Read each riddle. Look on the lily pad to search for each answer. Write it on the line.

1. What does your mom want in your room?
   _____ *less mess* _____

2. How does a snake say I love you? _____

3. What do you call a big pile of clothes in your closet?
   _____

4. What do you call it when you are being very quiet?
   _____

5. What do you call a cup for an ant? _____

6. What do you call fake hair for a hog? _____

7. How does Mama Frog wash her floor? _____

8. What do you call a dog mug? _____

9. Where can you learn to fix windows? _____

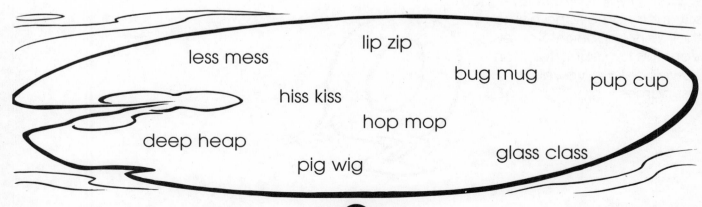

less mess

lip zip

bug mug

pup cup

hiss kiss

hop mop

deep heap

glass class

pig wig

Reviewing Vowel Sounds

The No-Vowel Challenge

Write a consonant-vowel-consonant (CVC) word such as *bat* on the board without the vowel and challenge students to try to say it. Invite other students to listen for the vowel the volunteer provides when trying to read the word. Invite students to name all the CVC words that can be made using the those letters. For *b __ t*, examples could would be *bat*, *bet*, *bit*, *bot*, and *but*.

Stay Up, Sit Down

Invite students to stand by their chairs. Slowly read a list of single-syllable words. If the word has a long vowel, players stand or remain standing. If it has a short vowel, they sit down. For a decoding variation, show flashcards instead of reading the list aloud. Invite the group to read the card aloud after they stand or sit. For a quieter version, have students raise their hands for long vowels and lower them for short vowels.

VIV (Very Important Vowels)

Invite students who have long vowels in their first names to line up first. As they walk to get into line, have them say their names and name their very important vowels. Vary this by asking for short vowels or long vowels in last names.

Vowel Scrapbooks

Invite students to find pictures of objects that have long vowel sounds in old magazines or catalogs and cut them out. Encourage them to paste each picture on a separate sheet of paper and label it. Then have the students write silly stories that include their selections. Staple each set of story and picture pages together to make books. Divide the class into small groups and allow time for the young authors to share their creations.

Read Alouds

Take your class to the school library and point out the section that features easy-readers and early chapter books. Select one or two titles to read aloud, and then encourage students to choose their own. A few suggested titles are listed below.

The Sneetches and Other Stories by Dr. Seuss

Are You My Mother? by P. D. Eastman

Henry and Mudge: The First Book by Cynthia Rylant

Arthur Babysits by Marc Brown

 **Phonics**

What's Missing?

Directions: Look at each picture. Write the missing vowel on the line.

| a | e | o |

1. n <u>e</u> t

2. p _ n

3. h _ t

4. b _ t

5. b _ ll

6. w _ ll

7. w _ ll

8. d _ g

9. r _ t

10. c _ b

11. b _ x

12. h _ nd

0-7424-2832-X *Reading for Every Child: Phonics*

My Dog and I

Directions: Read each sentence. Circle the word that makes sense.

1. My dog likes to (**beg, jet**).

2. My dog (**cup, dug**) a big hole.

3. Dogs like to (**fun, tug**) on ropes.

4. I (**fed, jet**) my dog.

5. I had to (**hot, mop**) up his mess.

6. My dog got dirt on the (**bug, rug**).

7. My dog has (**red, tell**) fur like a fox.

8. The dog ate my (**hut, lunch**)!

9. I like to (**tub, hug**) my dog.

10. My dog pants when he is (**doll, hot**).

11. My dog likes to sleep on my (**bed, well**).

12. It is my (**log, job**) to feed and walk the dog.

The Best Nest

Directions: Read the clues. Look at the words in the nest. Write the word in the puzzle.

nip   nut   mop
tan   dip   ten
tag   rat   win
nest   dog   top
set

Across

1. He wants to _____ the race.
4. I can count to _____.
6. She watched the _____ spin.
7. Please _____ the table.
9. It's time to feed the _____.
10. The _____ likes to eat cheese.
11. The cat tried to _____ my hand.

Down

2. The chipmunk is eating a _____.
3. She used a _____ to clean the floor.
5. Six birds are in the _____.
6. Look at the price _____.
8. I colored the dress _____.
9. He took a _____ in the pool.

Use the Side Gate

Directions: Find and circle the words in the puzzle.

```
Y  O  U  D  A  T  E  C  N
D  G  A  M  E  I  D  A  A
I  G  T  T  Q  L  L  M  M
C  C  A  T  U  V  A  E  E
U  U  U  T  A  B  T  M  T
T  S  T  B  E  M  E  T  E
U  M  E  E  E  M  E  W  T
N  X  M  H  A  T  E  L  D
E  J  U  N  E  S  A  M  E
```

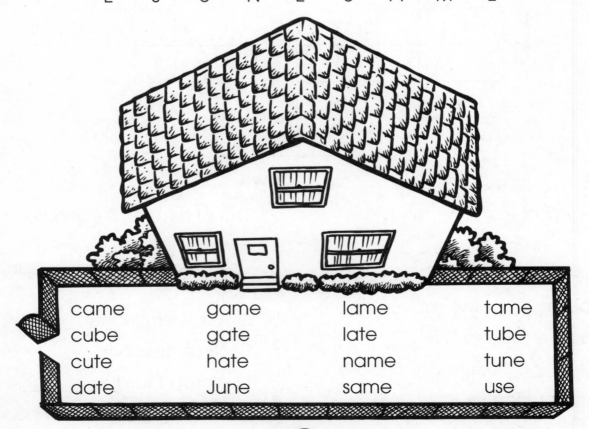

came	game	lame	tame
cube	gate	late	tube
cute	hate	name	tune
date	June	same	use

Phonics

My Code

Directions: Find out what the note says. Use the key to write the missing letter on each line. Then reread the letter.

Key:

1 = o   2 = e   3 = i

Hi, J__ __ ,
    1   2

    I h__p__ you can read this n__t__. I wr__t__ it in
        1 2   1 2   1 2

c__d__. I will call you on the ph__n__ later.
1 2   1 2

    I have a new j__k__ to tell you. It is about a m__l__
               1 2   1 2

in a h__l__. I heard it from M__k__. He came to my house
    1 2   3 2

on his new b__k__. It is very n__c__. He r__d__ almost a
           3 2   3 2   1 2

m__l__ to get here.
3 2

    When I get my b__k__, you and I can r__d__ to the
                 3 2   3 2

park. We can take a h__k__. We can play h__d__ and
               3 2   3 2

seek. We can go down the sl__d__.
                      3 2

    I will save my d__m__s to buy __c__ cream
               3 2   3 2

c__n__s. We will have a f__n__ t__m__! Did you l__k__
1 2   3 2   3 2   3 2

my n__t__? Please wr__t__ back!
   1 2   1 2

                      Your pal,

                      __k__
                      3 2

0-7424-2832-X *Reading for Every Child: Phonics*

Up on the Hill

Directions: Read each word. Color the words with long vowels **green**. Color the words with short vowels **yellow**.

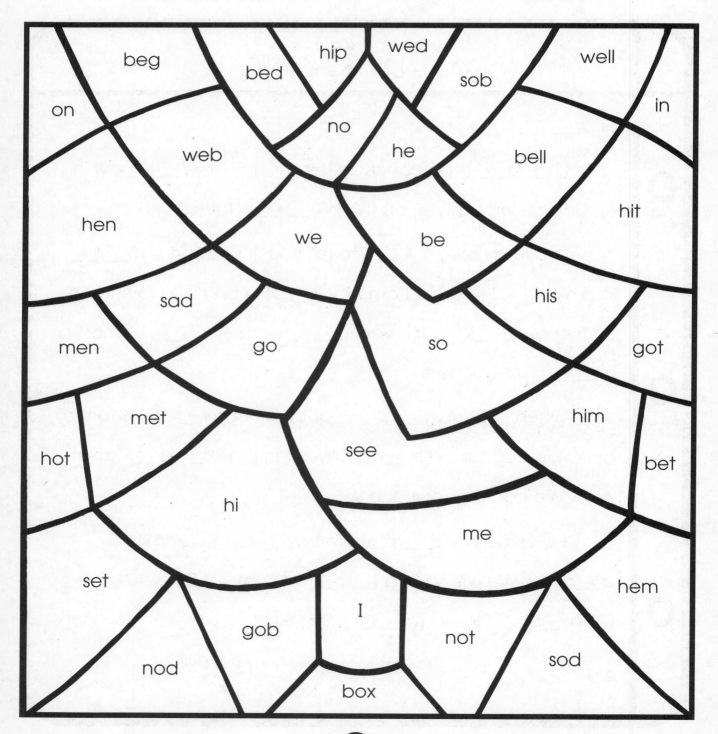

A Day Riddle

Directions: Read each sentence. Look in the Word Bank.
Write the letters to the answer on each line.

1. I will go _____ my father.   __ __ ☐ __

2. She will _____ for her team.   __ ☐ __ __ __

3. He likes his dog very _____.   __ ☐ __ __

4. She liked the _____ one.   __ __ __ ☐

5. I picked _____ one.   __ __ __ ☐

6. We fell into the _____.   ☐ __ __ __ __

7. I grew more _____ an inch.   __ __ ☐ __

8. _____ are coming over.   __ __ ☐ __

Word Bank			
they	much	other	than
cheer	with	this	ditch

Riddle:

If today is Thursday, what is the day after yesterday?

To find the answer, write each of the boxed letters
above on the lines in order. (Hint: It starts with a
capital letter.)

____ ____ ____ ____ ____ ____ ____ ____ ____

Whale of a Word

Directions: Find and circle the hidden words.

```
A  S  L  W  H  Y  W  P  H  A
W  B  H  S  H  W  H  A  T  E
T  H  R  A  H  I  A  K  N  Q
S  W  E  Q  R  O  L  L  N  S
W  H  Z  R  W  E  E  E  J  H
H  E  U  Q  E  H  W  L  S  O
I  N  N  T  D  N  E  F  H  R
C  S  H  A  P  E  G  E  E  T
H  T  S  H  O  W  K  Z  L  C
S  H  I  P  W  K  G  P  L  L
```

shape	shoe	whale	where
share	short	what	which
shell	show	wheel	while
ship	shut	when	why

Riddle:

What word has the most letters?

To find the answer, write the first ten letters from the puzzle that are not circled on the lines above. Write them in order from left to right, row by row.

___ ___ ___ ___ ___ ___ ___ ___ ___ ___

Scrambled!

Directions: Read each clue. Unscramble the word. Write it on the line.

1. the largest animal on Earth   aelwh _____

2. a big boat   pihs _____

3. found by the sea   llshes _____

4. what we do with our food   hcwe _____

5. used to steer a car or a boat   eewhl _____

6. what you wear on your feet   esohs _____

7. this word asks about a time   hwne _____

8. this tells what comes next   nthe _____

9. this can pay the bills   ckche _____

10. found on a bed   eshet _____

when   sheet   whale   wheel   then

shells chew   shoes   check

ship

Phonics

Castles

Directions: Color the castle piece **blue** if the word starts with a hard **c** (like **car**). Color the castle **orange** if it starts with a soft **c** (like **city**).

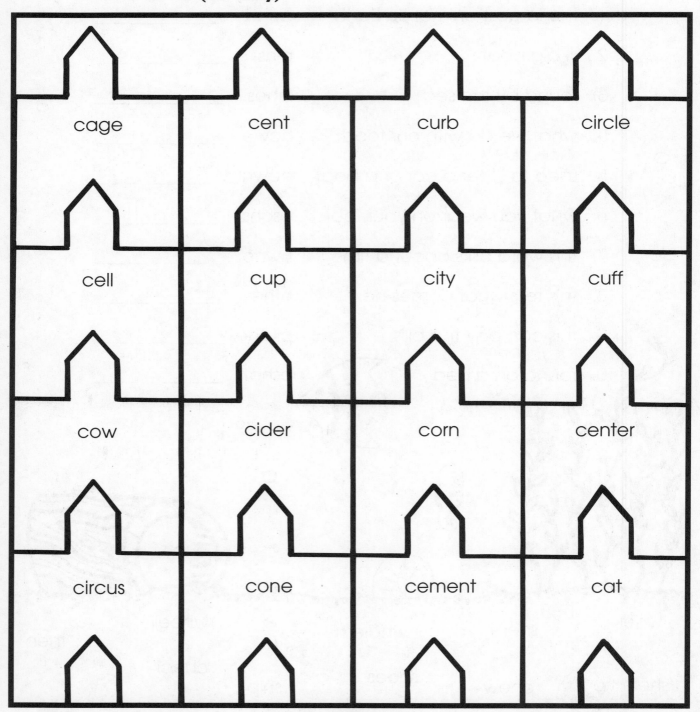

cage cent curb circle

cell cup city cuff

cow cider corn center

circus cone cement cat

0-7424-2832-X *Reading for Every Child: Phonics*

Who Is Hiding in the Trees?

Directions: Color the shape **yellow** if the word starts with a soft **g** (like **page**). Color the shape **brown** if the word starts with a hard **g** (like **go**).

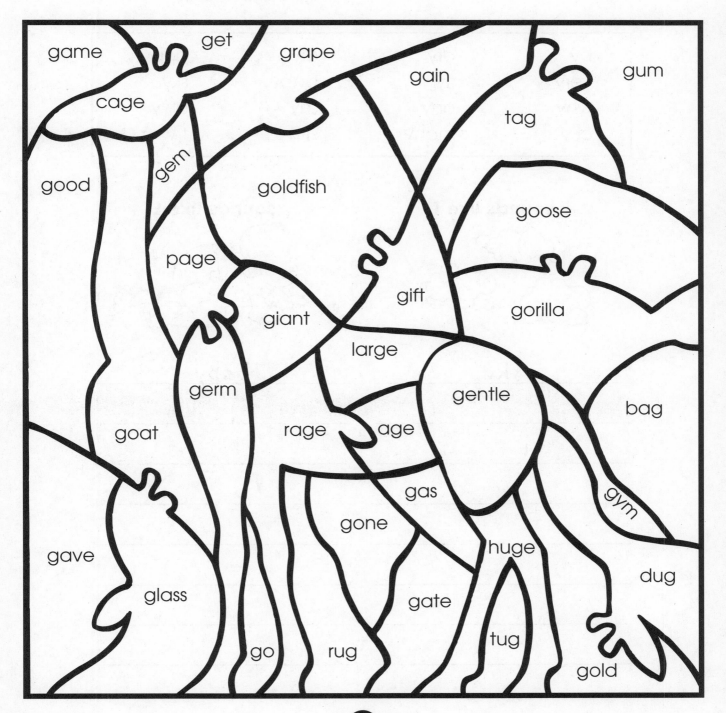

Phonics

E or I?

Directions: What sound does the letter **y** make in these words? Write each word in the correct column. The first one is done for you.

by	dry	my	copy
very	fly	baby	sky
why	any	shy	only
city	many	story	try

y sounds like I   **y sounds like E**

_____ sky _____   _____ baby _____

_____   _____

_____   _____

_____   _____

_____   _____

_____   _____

_____   _____

Free Time

Directions: Fill in the bubble for the word that makes sense in each sentence.

1. I like to ride in the _____.   ○ cat   ○ can   ○ car

2. I take my bike to the _____.   ○ pick   ○ park   ○ pink

3. It is not very _____ away.   ○ far   ○ fat   ○ fall

4. I like to wear my _____.   ○ slim   ○ slippers   ○ stern

5. He likes to play in the _____.   ○ yam   ○ year   ○ yard

6. Our cat chews on the _____.   ○ fun   ○ fern   ○ fast

7. My dog likes to run and _____.   ○ bark   ○ book   ○ bank

8. We walked over to _____ house.   ○ hen   ○ her   ○ hem

9. Our yard is fun after _____.   ○ drink   ○ ding   ○ dark

10. I make a wish on the first _____.   ○ star   ○ stay   ○ stand

11. We try to play _____.   ○ hat   ○ head   ○ hard

12. I keep my bugs in a _____.   ○ jar   ○ jet   ○ jog

     0-7424-2832-X *Reading for Every Child: Phonics*

 **Phonics**

Stirring the Soup

Directions: Read the words on the pot. Write the matching word for each picture.

1. ____bird____

2. _____

3. _____

4. _____

5. _____

6. _____

7. _____

8. _____

9. _____

10. _____

11. _____

12. _____

nurse	horn	cord
fork	fur	thorn
storm	corn	bird
skirt	shirt	curl

 30

 **Phonics**

A Sweet Treat

Directions: Look at the picture and read the choices. Write the word that matches each picture on the line.

1.
   pike
   poke
   peak

   _____peak_____

2.
   peel
   pill
   pale

   _____

3.
   rode
   ride
   read

   _____

4.
   said
   seed
   sit

   _____

5.
   shop
   shape
   sheep

   _____

6.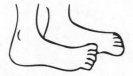
   fit
   feet
   fat

   _____

7.
   pie
   paw
   peas

   _____

8.
   try
   true
   tree

   _____

9.
   cheek
   check
   chick

   _____

10.
    peach
    pitch
    poach

    _____

11.
    quick
    quiz
    queen

    _____

12.
    sale
    seal
    sole

    _____

 **Phonics**

Beetlerella's Bug Ball

Directions: Read each riddle and the phrases in the box below. Write the answer on the line.

1. What do you call a flock of fireflies? _glow show_

2. What do you call a big black bird on the ground?

   _____

3. What do you call a jacket to wear on a ship?

   _____

4. What do you call a ski race? _____

5. What took Beetlerella to the Bug Ball?

   _____

6. What football game is played underground?

   _____

7. What do you call it when you heat bread over a campfire?

   _____

8. What do you call a life jacket?

   _____

9. What do you call a bullfrog bath? _____

low crow	boat coat	roach coach
snow show	toast roast	float coat
Mole Bowl	croak soak	glow show

Inching Along

Directions: Read each word. Color the space **yellow** if the word has the long **a** sound (like **day**). Color the space **purple** if the word has a short **a** sound (like **apple**).

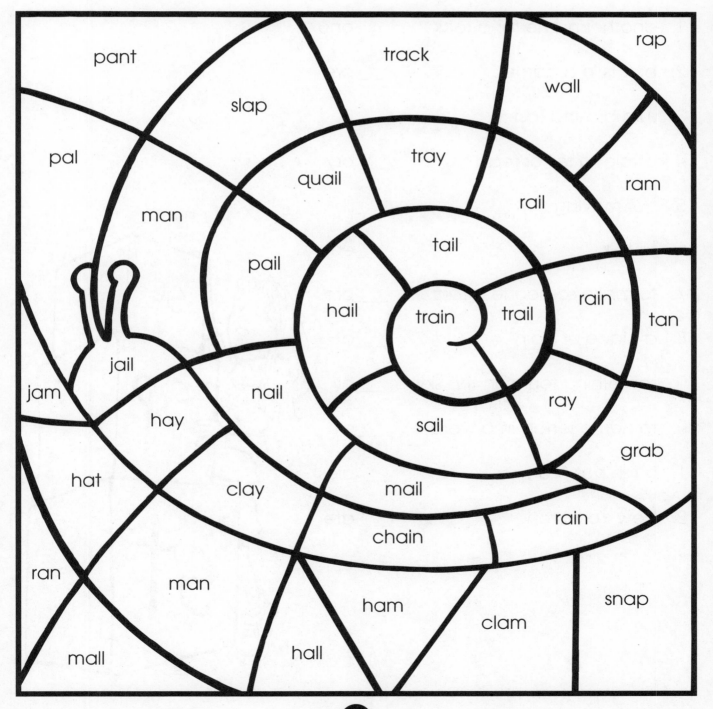

Stack and Spell

Directions: Read each clue. Write **sc**, **st**, or **sp** on the line to complete the word.

1. another name for a rock   ____one

2. points in a game   ____ore

3. turn around fast   ____in

4. a tale to tell or read   ____ory

5. not moving   ____ill

6. to talk   ____eak

7. to make someone afraid   ____are

8. a place or stain   ____ot

9. something found in the sky   ____ar

10. to name letters in a word   ____ell

11. a fish has many   ____ales

12. New York is one   ____ate

Phonics

Fish School

Directions: Read each riddle and the shells below. Write the answer to the riddle on the line.

1. What do you call a very dark bag? _____

2. What's another name for telling on each other?

   _____

3. What do you call a flower shop? _____

4. What do you call the father of a good student?

   _____

5. What do you call baby bear pals?

   _____

6. What do you call a stone sun dial?

   _____

7. Where do fish learn? _____

8. What do you call a knee slap? _____

9. What do you a cat that's running fast?

   _____

lap slap
cub club
purr blur

blame game
black sack
glad dad

bloom room
rock clock
bass class

0-7424-2832-X *Reading for Every Child: Phonics*

A Slippery Puzzle

Directions: Read each clue. Write **fl**, **pl**, or **sl** in the puzzle to complete the answers.

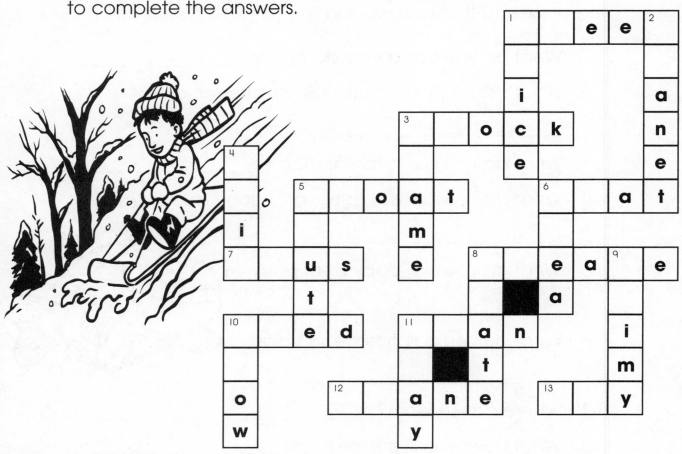

Across

1. We do this at night.
3. A group of birds.
5. A boat can do this.
6. It has no bumps.
7. You say this when you add.
8. Say this when you ask.
10. It slides down a snowy hill.
11. Do this before a trip.
12. It takes us into the sky.
13. A plane can do this.

Down

1. A piece of bread
2. Earth is one and so is Mars.
3. Part of a fire.
4. Fall down.
5. Blow on this to play a tune.
6. This bug is in a very small circus.
8. This is another name for a dish.
9. A slug feels like this.
10. Not fast.
11. Have fun or make music.

Crab Walk

Directions: Use one of the blends on the crabs to finish each word.

 fr

 br

 cr

dr

1. _____aw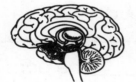

2. _____ain

3. _____own

4. _____um

5. _____og

6. _____ead

7. _____ess

8. _____ush

9. _____ip

10. _____ame

11. _____ow

12. _____uit

0-7424-2832-X *Reading for Every Child: Phonics*

Train Tracks

Directions: Write the missing word on the line.

track	tree	train	try

1. My dad and I have a model _____.

2. He has more than just trains and a _____.

3. Last night he made a toy pine _____.

4. Now he wants me to _____ to make one.

trade	press	proud	price

5. I learned how to _____ the parts together.

6. I would not sell that house for any _____.

7. I am very _____ of our hard work.

8. My friend wants to _____ a tunnel for it.

grass	green	grow	grin

9. I just _____ and shake my head.

10. I put some _____ on our hills last night.

11. It is _____ and looks real.

12. I wish it would _____ by itself.

One Knight's Knots

Directions: Write **kn** or **wr** in each space to complete the word. Then write the word on the line.

1. Our ball team is called the __kn__ights.   _____knights_____

2. Jack, our star player, hurt his _____ee.   _____

3. He scraped his _____uckle too.   _____

4. He had a big purple _____ot on his head.   _____

5. Worst of all, he broke his _____ist.   _____

6. We saw our coach _____eel down beside him.   _____

7. The coach had to _____ap up his wrist.   _____

8. Now Jack has to _____ite with his other hand.   _____

9. His doctor _____ote a note to our coach.   _____

10. Everyone _____ows he is our best player.   _____

11. He can _____ock the ball out of the park.   _____

12. Playing without him just feels _____ong.   _____

Phonics

Spring Flowers

Directions: Write **str**, **spr**, or **spl** on each line in the first column to make the word match the clue. Then write the whole word.

Word Part	Clues	Answer
1. _spl_ash	when you hit the water	splash
2. ____ay	to squirt	
3. ____ap	holds things in place	
4. ____ange	odd or not known	
5. ____inter	a bit of wood in your finger	
6. ____aw	use this to sip	
7. ____ing	it comes after winter	
8. ____eet	a city road	
9. ____it	to crack or break	
10. ____out	start to grow	
11. ____ing	use this to tie things	
12. ____ong	not weak	

Phonics _____ final consonant blends (nk, nt, st)

A Trip to the Bank

Directions: Write **nk**, **nt**, or **st** on the line to finish each sentence.

1. I we_____ to the bank last Friday.

2. I keep some money in the ba_____.

3. I had to hu_____ for my bank book.

4. I was afraid it was lo_____.

5. I had to pri_____ my name.

6. It's hard to write in i_____.

7. I know mo_____ of the tellers.

8. My grandmother se_____ me a check.

9. I used mo_____ of the money to buy a game.

10. It co_____ seven dollars and twenty cents.

11. I saved the re_____ of the money.

12. I put it in the ba_____.

The Old Tower

Directions: Read each sentence and the words in the bank. Write a word on the line to finish each sentence.

1. I went with my dad to an _____ bell tower.

2. A _____ man met us at the door.

3. He had a _____ in one hand.

4. It was warm outside but _____ inside.

5. It was _____ and moldy in the tower.

6. I am glad I wasn't by _____.

7. We saw a _____ on the wall.

8. It held a letter in a _____ frame.

9. There was a _____ on the letter.

10. The man _____ us about the letter.

11. It was written by a _____.

12. I jumped when I heard a strange _____.

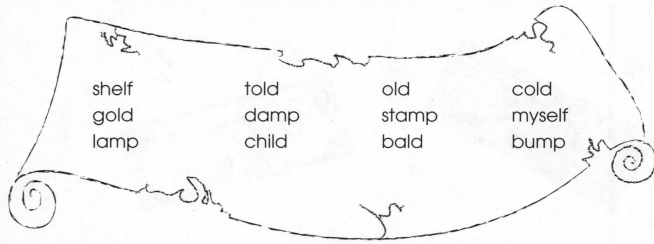

shelf	told	old	cold
gold	damp	stamp	myself
lamp	child	bald	bump

Down for the Count

Directions: Write each word in the correct family.

shout   brown
growl   howl
couch   frown   down
clown   sound   bounce
proud

ou family   **ow family**

_____   _____

_____   _____

_____   _____

_____   _____

_____   _____

_____   _____

0-7424-2832-X *Reading for Every Child: Phonics*

Ship Ahoy!

Directions: Read each sentence and the words under water. Write the word that makes sense in the sentence.

1. She found a shiny _____ on the playground.

2. He was the only _____ at the table.

3. I cleared my _____ before I started to sing.

4. We had a _____ of pizza or soup for dinner.

5. Grandma bought me a _____ for my birthday.

6. She put the _____ in the flower pot first.

7. He wrapped the rest of his meal in _____.

8. I heard a loud _____ coming from her room.

9. He jumped for _____ when he won the race.

10. The _____ of the pencil was really sharp.

11. Would you like to _____ our group?

12. I waited for the water to _____.

---

foil	choice	coin	noise
soil	toy	join	joy
voice	boy	point	boil

A Good Book

Directions: Read each sentence. Circle each word that has the letter pair **oo**. Then write the circled words on the correct page in the book below.

1. Look up at the sky.

2. We eat lunch at noon.

3. I saw the full moon.

4. She chopped all the wood.

5. They have a messy room.

6. I hurt my foot when I fell.

7. He took his time walking home.

8. Please put up your hood.

9. We're going to the zoo today.

10. The goose was in the pond.

11. That is a great book.

12. You have a new tooth.

Sounds like **took**

_____

_____

_____

_____

_____

Sounds like **moon**

_____

_____

_____

_____

_____

Shining at Night

Directions: Say each word. Color the piece **blue** if it sounds like **book**. Color it **yellow** if it sounds like **broom**.

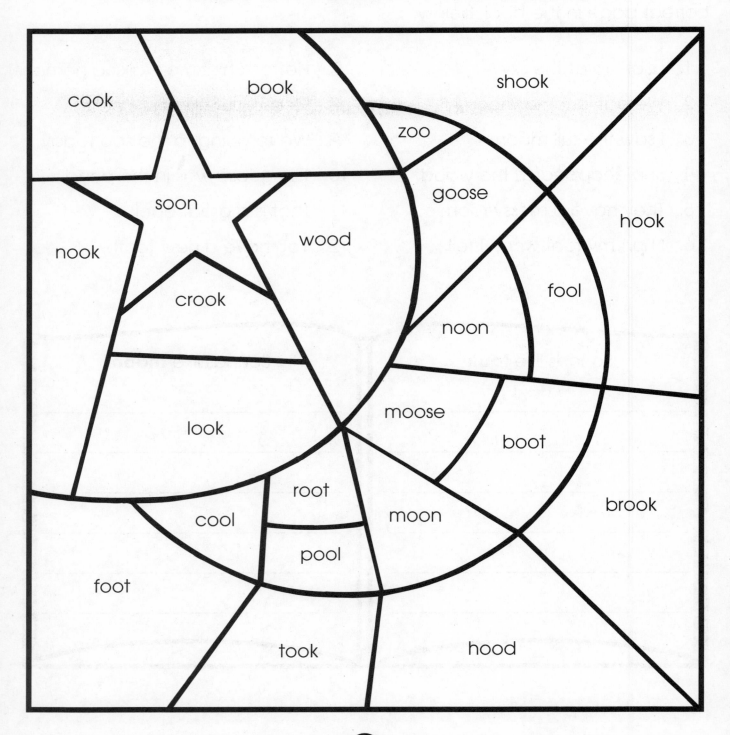

Blast Off!

Directions: Read each word. Color the piece **red** if the word has a long **i** sound (like **night**). Color the space **blue** if the word has short **i** sound (like **dip**).

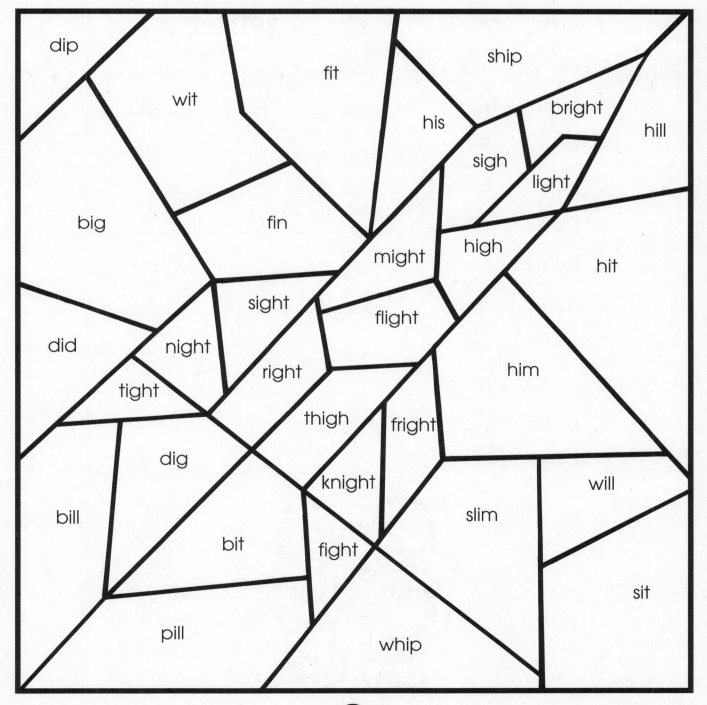

Compound Words

Directions: Draw a line from a word in the first column to a word in the second column to make a compound word. Write the new word on the line.

1.	bath	noon	bathtub
2.	air	stairs	_____
3.	after	tub	_____
4.	down	light	_____
5.	base	berry	_____
6.	blue	father	_____
7.	butter	plane	_____
8.	day	one	_____
9.	any	ball	_____
10.	grand	house	_____
11.	home	work	_____
12.	light	fly	_____

0-7424-2832-X *Reading for Every Child: Phonics*

Everything, Except Onions

Directions: Make a compound word using the words in the sandwiches and the words in the box. Write the compound words on the lines.

body	where	one	thing

1.

2.
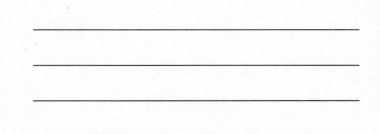

3.

Play Ball!

Directions: Combine each base word with **ball** to make a compound word. Write the new word on the line.

Base Word   +   ball

1. basket _____

2. base _____

3. foot _____

4. kick _____

5. fast _____

6. hand _____

7. snow _____

8. meat _____

9. soft _____

10. volley _____

Rays of Sunshine

Directions: Make compound words by adding **sun** to beginning of each word below. Write the compound words on the lines.

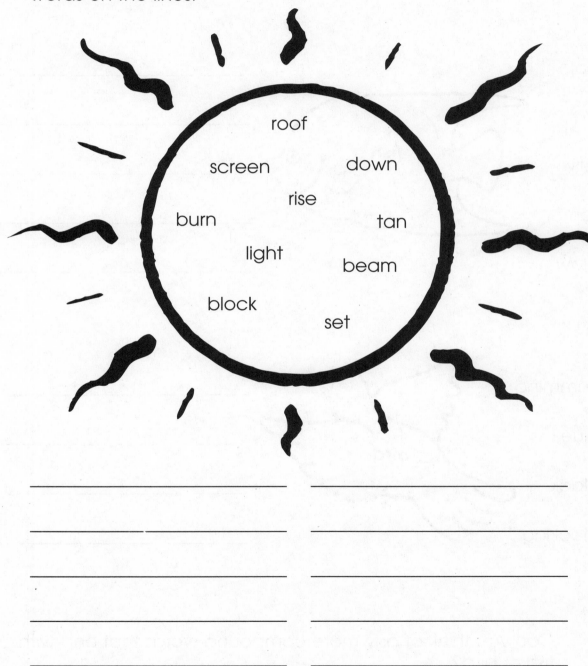

roof

screen   down

rise

burn   tan

light

beam

block

set

_____   _____

_____   _____

_____   _____

_____   _____

Compound Critters

Directions: Combine each word with the one on the picture. Write the new compound word on the line.

1. gold

2. star

3. jelly

4. lion

5. blow

_____

_____

_____

_____

_____

6. humming

7. blue

8. black

9. mocking

_____

_____

_____

_____

Can you think of any more compound words that end with fish or bird?

0-7424-2832-X *Reading for Every Child: Phonics*

Compound Words Puzzle

Directions: Read the clues. Write the compound words in the puzzle.

Across

1. a flake of snow
4. a place to sleep
5. a cone with pine seeds inside
7. a wild cat
9. when the sun goes down
10. a bug with pretty wings

Down

2. where planes land
3. time after morning
6. a sea animal that looks like jelly
7. a game with three bases and a home plate
8. reading or writing to do at home

Breaking It Down

Clap It Out

Say a word with two or more syllables. The word "syllable" is a good starting word. Invite the class to repeat after you. Say the word one syllable at a time and clap once for each. Have the students repeat. Say it at normal speed, keeping the claps and have students repeat. Good sources for words include stories that you are reading aloud to the class, science and social studies projects, and special school events.

Two Fingers, Three Fingers, Four

Say a word. Encourage students to raise their hands and indicate the number of syllables with their fingers. Include familiar words with two, three, and four syllables. Start with things in the classroom such as cupboard, table, computer, and window. Move out to include such words as neighborhood, automobile, and telephone.

Read Alouds

Second graders enjoy listening to stories that are beyond their reading ability. Try E. B. White's classics *Charlotte's Web* and *Stuart Little*, Beverly Cleary's hilarious stories about Henry Huggins and his irrepressible little friend Ramona, and Louis Sachar's *Sideways Stories of Wayside School*. Select polysyllabic words from these readings to expand students' vocabulary.

Two-Syllable Stand-Up

Read a mixed list of one-, two-, and three-syllable words. Challenge students to stand when they hear a two-syllable word and sit down when they hear a word with any other number of syllables. This may also be played as three-syllable stand-up.

Chant the Syl-la, Syl-la, Syl-lables

Say a three-syllable word, such as *acrobat*. Invite students to make it into a chant by repeating the first two syllables twice, then adding the third. Acrobat would become: "ac-ro, ac-ro, ac-ro-bat." Add a refrain, such as "That is what we say." You may make this into a memory game by having the students repeat all of the words you have given them in a session. After they learn the game, they may offer three-syllable words of their own.

Ig-Pay Atin-Lay

Remember Pig Latin? It actually helped generations of kids learn to hear and manipulate syllables. If you're rusty, here are the rules. Take the first letter off of any word. Put it at the end and add long /a/ to form a new syllable. "Pig" becomes "ig-pay." Once children start this, they won't need much encouragement.

Feel the Beat

Directions: Write the number of syllables you hear in each word.

1. bee ___1___	7. ladder _____
2. toothpaste _____	8. pinecone _____
3. tunnel _____	9. TODAY'S LESSON: chalkboard _____
4. umbrella _____	10. butterfly _____
5. strawberry _____	11. baseball _____
6. train _____	12. basketball _____

0-7424-2832-X *Reading for Every Child: Phonics*

Phonics

Dividing Syllables

Directions: Circle the double consonants in each word. Then circle the choice that is divided correctly.

1. **cotton**   co/tton   cott/on   ~~cot/ton~~

2. **supper**   sup/per   su/pper   supp/er

3. **arrow**   arr/ow   ar/row   a/rrow

4. **allow**   a/llow   all/ow   al/low

5. **common**   co/mmon   com/mon   comm/on

6. **hammer**   ham/mer   ha/mmer   hamm/er

7. **ladder**   ladd/er   lad/der   la/dder

8. **arrive**   a/rrive   arr/ive   ar/rive

9. **tunnel**   tun/nel   tunn/el   tu/nnel

10. **narrow**   na/rrow   nar/row   narr/ow

11. **valley**   vall/ey   va/lley   val/ley

12. **willow**   will/ow   wil/low   wi/llow

Chipmunk's Challenge

Directions: Say and clap each word. The syllables break between the consonants. Fill in the bubble of the word divided correctly.

Example: **chipmunk**   ○ chi/pmunk   ○ chipm/unk   ● chip/munk

1.	**almond**	○ a/lmond	○ al/mond	○ alm/ond
2.	**cartoon**	○ cart/oon	○ ca/rtoon	○ car/toon
3.	**chimney**	○ chi/mney	○ chim/ney	○ chimn/ey
4.	**thirteen**	○ thir/teen	○ thi/rteen	○ thirt/een
5.	**market**	○ mar/ket	○ ma/rket	○ mark/et
6.	**garden**	○ gard/en	○ ga/rden	○ gar/den
7.	**number**	○ num/ber	○ nu/mber	○ numb/er
8.	**circus**	○ circ/us	○ ci/rcus	○ cir/cus
9.	**monkey**	○ mo/nkey	○ mon/key	○ monk/ey
10.	**umpire**	○ um/pire	○ u/mpire	○ ump/ire
11.	**welcome**	○ we/lcome	○ wel/come	○ welc/ome
12.	**window**	○ wi/ndow	○ wind/ow	○ win/dow

⊛ **Phonics**   inflectional endings (ing, ed, s)

Taking a Walk

Directions: Write the **s**, **ed**, and **ing** forms of each word.
The first one is done for you.

Example: **walk** _____*walks*_____   _____*walked*_____   _____*walking*_____

1. talk   _____   _____   _____

2. wait   _____   _____   _____

3. play   _____   _____   _____

4. laugh   _____   _____   _____

5. whisper   _____   _____   _____

6. work   _____   _____   _____

7. turn   _____   _____   _____

8. print   _____   _____   _____

9. open   _____   _____   _____

10. clean   _____   _____   _____

11. stay   _____   _____   _____

12. wonder   _____   _____   _____

**Phonics**

Wolfs or Wolves?

Rules:

When a word ends with *y*, the *y* changes to *i* before the ending is added.

When a word ends with one *f*, change the *f* to a **v** before adding the ending.

When a word ends with *x*, *v*, *ch*, or *sh*, add an **e** before adding an **s**.

Directions: Read each sentence. Write the correct plural on the line.

1. I packed both _____.	lunchs	lunches
2. The _____ are dirty.	dishs	dishes
3. He carried the three _____.	boxes	boxs
4. I like to visit big _____.	citys	cities
5. I have ten _____ in my pocket.	pennies	pennys
6. He made three _____.	wishs	wishes
7. We sat on the park _____.	benches	benchs
8. I have two _____ of bread.	loaves	loafs
9. We picked a basket of _____.	berries	berrys
10. He raked the _____.	leaves	leafs
11. I heard the _____ howling.	wolfs	wolves

Adding Endings

A suffix is a syllable that is added to the end of a word. It adds to the word's meaning or changes the meaning in some way.

The suffix **-ful** means *full of*.
The suffix **-less** means *without*.
The suffix **-er** means *more*.
The suffix **-est** means the *most*.

Directions: Add a suffix to each word to make it match the clue.

Base Word	Clue	New Word
1. clear	more clear	*clearer*
2. kind	the most kind	_____
3. color	without color	_____
4. hope	full of hope	_____
5. power	full of power	_____
6. small	more small	_____
7. care	without care	_____
8. neat	the most neat	_____
9. quick	more quick	_____
10. wonder	full of wonder	_____

A Bushel of Apples

Directions: Write the plural form of each word.

girl
1.

dog
2.

table
3.

chair
4.

room
5.

desk
6.

door
7.

book
8.

pencil
9.

ruler
10.

marker
11.

window
12.

One Sheep, Two Sheep

Directions: Draw a line to match each word to its plural.

1. leaf   children
2. wolf   knives
3. child   leaves
4. knife   wolves

5. woman   sheep
6. deer   deer
7. man   men
8. sheep   women

9. mouse   feet
10. foot   mice
11. goose   teeth
12. tooth   geese

 **Phonics**

The Dog's Bone

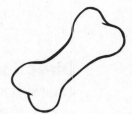

Directions: Draw a line to match each possessive to its meaning.

1.	boy's	belongs to a cat
2.	girl's	belongs to a boy
3.	dog's	belongs to a girl
4.	cat's	belongs to a dog

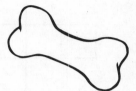

5.	pig's	belongs to a frog
6.	bird's	belongs to a cow
7.	frog's	belongs to a pig
8.	cow's	belongs to a bird

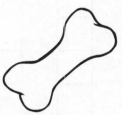

9.	knight's	belongs to a mouse
10.	friend's	belongs to a duck
11.	mouse's	belongs to a friend
12.	duck's	belongs to a knight

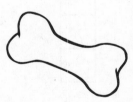

Untidy Room

Directions: Read each clue. Write the answer in the crossword puzzle. Remember: *re* means **again** and *un* means **not**.

Across

1. not true
5. make new again
7. not able
8. live again
10. not made
11. take again
12. paint again

Down

2. not paid
3. not happy
4. heat again
6. run or show again
7. not colored
8. make again
9. write again
10. not tied

You're a Winner!

Directions: Write the word that belongs on each line.

1. They ____*aren't*____ home yet.

2. That _____ my dog.

3. I _____ seen him.

4. He _____ done his work.

5. She _____ there.

6. I _____ eat that candy.

7. They _____ happy.

8. They _____ do it again.

9. He _____ like apples.

10. He _____ tell me the secret.

11. She _____ done anything.

12. We _____ coming.

Phonics

I'll Call You Later

Directions: Complete each sentence. Use a word from the box.

That's	She'll

1. _____ be late.

2. _____ not true.

There's	He'll

3. _____ only one left.

4. _____ give it to you.

He's	I'll

5. _____ up first.

6. _____ meet you there.

We'll	He's

7. _____ the only one here.

8. _____ do the work for you.

They'll	She's

9. _____ the first one in line.

10. _____ give you a ride home.

We'll	It's

11. _____ your turn.

12. _____ play after school.

Here's	They'll

13. _____ your book.

14. _____ come over tomorrow.

What's	I'll

15. _____ call you later.

16. _____ that movie about?

Phonics

Two Peas in a Pod

Directions: Complete each sentence. Use a word from the box.

| two |
| too |

1. There were _____ deer in the yard.
2. I saw them _____.

| too |
| to |

3. We went _____ the mall.
4. He is _____ little to go with you.

| know |
| no |

5. My mom said _____.
6. I _____ how to ride a bike.

| knew |
| new |

7. I have a _____ bike.
8. I _____ I would like it.

| two |
| to |

9. The number _____ comes after one.
10. I want _____ come with you.

| know |
| no |

11. There are _____ boys here.
12. I _____ those two boys.

| knew |
| new |

13. That is a _____ book.
14. I _____ I could read it.

Dear Deer

Directions: Complete each sentence.
Write a word from the box.

| deer |
| dear |

1. The _____ ate grass.
2. She is a _____ friend.

3. I will _____ you at the mall.
4. Chicken is my favorite _____.

| meat |
| meet |

| beat |
| beet |

5. His face was as red as a _____.
6. He likes to _____ the drum.

7. I saw three _____ in the woods.
8. Grandma is _____ to me.

| dear |
| deer |

| meat |
| meet |

9. I like to _____ new people.
10. You have to cook _____.

11. I will _____ him at checkers.
12. My mom boiled the _____.

| beat |
| beet |

| meet |
| meat |

13. We had _____ for supper.
14. He wanted to _____ me.

Missing Marks

Directions: In each sentence, there is one misspelled word and a missing punctuation mark. Cross out the misspelled word and write the correct word above it. Write the punctuation mark in the box (**. ? !**).

1. Do you ~~no~~ _know_ where it is [**?**]

2. I know how two do that [ ]

3. The big bare is coming [ ]

4. Who is hear today [ ]

5. We one the game [ ]

6. Bee nice to your sister [ ]

7. What rode do you live on [ ]

8. The table is made out of would [ ]

9. My little brother is won year old [ ]

10. He road the horse down the street [ ]

11. Are we going the write way [ ]

12. Get away from the be [ ]

Fill-It-In Puzzle

Directions: Count the boxes for each word. Look in that letter list for a word that might fit. Write the word in the puzzle. (Hint: Start with the word already written in and work your way left.)

4-letter words
been
read
said

5-letter words
again
could
their
where

6-letter words
always
please
school

7-letter words
another
because

Morning ABCs

Directions: Color the circle in front of the word that comes first in abc order.

1. ○ been
   ● always
   ○ color

2. ○ other
   ○ been
   ○ some

3. ○ have
   ○ know
   ○ never

4. ○ its
   ○ color
   ○ good

5. ○ read
   ○ some
   ○ under

6. ○ morning
   ○ know
   ○ other

7. ○ people
   ○ read
   ○ have

8. ○ some
   ○ found
   ○ never

9. ○ under
   ○ morning
   ○ would

10. ○ their
    ○ some
    ○ would

11. ○ been
    ○ good
    ○ some

12. ○ never
    ○ morning
    ○ know

Eight on My Plate

Directions: Look at the first word. Color in the circle for the word that rhymes with it .

1. white   ○ wit   ○ mitt   ● bright

2. high   ○ fry   ○ hit   ○ way

3. knight   ○ kite   ○ knit   ○ knot

4. try   ○ free   ○ may   ○ thigh

5. light   ○ bite   ○ treat   ○ bet

6. could   ○ bud   ○ pod   ○ wood

7. bead   ○ said   ○ red   ○ need

8. some   ○ roam   ○ gum   ○ home

9. should   ○ bold   ○ good   ○ bald

10. know   ○ go   ○ cow   ○ law

11. quite   ○ kit   ○ right   ○ cute

12. nail   ○ sigh   ○ so   ○ pale

13. write   ○ wet   ○ night   ○ wait

14. date   ○ eight   ○ that   ○ feet

0-7424-2832-X *Reading for Every Child: Phonics*

 **Phonics**

Friends to the End

Directions: Read the words in the box below. Then read the words that follow. Write a **synonym** (means the same) from the list for each word.

small	sleep	fast	shout
stack	land	speak	raise

1. ground   *land*

2. nap _____

3. talk _____

4. little _____

5. yell _____

6. lift _____

7. pile _____

8. quick _____

Directions: Read the words in the box below. Then read the words that follow. Write an **antonym** (opposite) from the list for each word.

cry	show	found	near
more	after	night	last

9. before   *after*

10. lost _____

11. first _____

12. far _____

13. laugh _____

14. hide _____

15. fewer _____

16. day _____

The Floating Hand

Directions: Read each question. Look at the book. Write the answer on the line.

1. What is the title of this book? _____

2. Who is the author? _____

3. What does an author do? _____

4. Who is the illustrator? _____

5. What does an illustrator do? _____

6. Is this a fiction or nonfiction book? _____

THE SLEEPOVER 5
BUMP IN THE NIGHT 11
THE FLOATING HAND 19
LOST AND FOUND 28
THE PROMISE 39

7. How many chapters are in this book? _____

8. What is the title of the second chapter? _____

9. On what page does "Lost and Found" start? _____

10. Would you want to read this book? Why? _____

Cultivating a Love of Reading

Great Book Series for Students

Amelia Bedelia books by Peggy Parish

Arthur books by Marc Brown

Berenstain Bears books by Stan & Jan Berenstain

Cam Jansen books by David Adler

Clifford books by Norman Bridwell

Curious George books by H. A. Rey

Franklin series by Paulette Bourgeois

Frog and Toad books by Arnold Lobel

Froggy books by Jonathan London

George and Martha books by James Marshall

Henry and Mudge books by Cynthia Rylant

Huggly books by Tedd Arnold

Junie B. Jones books by Barbara Park

A Little Critter Book series by Mercer Mayer

Little Bear books by Else Holmelund Minarik

Nate the Great books by Marjorie Sharmat

Pinky and Rex books by James Howe

Fun Teacher Read Alouds

A Light in the Attic by Shel Silverstein

Aaron's Hair by Robert Munsch

Bedhead by Margie Palatini

Click, Clack, Moo: Cows That Type by Doreen Cronin

Cloudy with a Chance of Meatballs by Judi Barrett

Diary of a Worm by Doreen Cronin

Dog Breath! The Horrible Trouble With Hally Tosis by Dav Pilkey

Double Trouble in Walla Walla by Andrew Clements

Falling Up by Shel Silverstein

Grandpa's Teeth by Rod Clement

Hooway for Wodney Wat by Helen Lester

I Know an Old Lady Who Swallowed a Pie by Alison Jackson

I'm Not Feeling Well Today by Shirley Neitzel

If Only I Had a Green Nose by Max Lucado

I'm a Manatee by John Lithgow

Judy Moody by Megan McDonald

Madeline by Ludwig Bemelmans

Magic Tree House series by Mary Pope Osborne

Miss Nelson Is Missing by Harry Allard

Paper Bag Princess by Michael Martchenko

Pickles to Pittsburg by Judi Barrett

Stellaluna by Janell Cannon

The Ant Bully by John Nickle

The Boxcar Children series by Gertrude Chandler Warner

The Incredible Shrinking Teacher by Lisa Passen

The Recess Queen by Alexis O' Neill

The Secret Garden by Frances Burnett

There Was an Old Lady Who Swallowed a Fly by Simms Taback

Tuesday by David Wiesner

Verdi by Janell Cannon

Walter, the Farting Dog by William Kotzwinkle

What Are YOU So Grumpy About? by Tom Lichtenheld

Where the Sidewalk Ends by Shel Silverstein

Resources for Reading Teachers

Reading about successful activities other teachers have used will help you tap into your own creativity as you teach reading. Here are some recommended teacher resources. The list includes books from the International Reading Association's Web site (www.reading.org).

A Poem a Day by Helen H. Moore

Alternatives to Worksheets by Karen Bauer and Rosa Drew

Creative Writing for Primary Grades by Scotty W. Price

Easy Lessons for Teaching Word Families by Judy Lynch

Getting Ready to Teach Second Grade by Kimberly Seto

If You're Trying to Teach Kids How to Write ... You've Gotta Have This Book by Marjorie Frank

Making More Words by Patricia M. Cunningham and Dorothy P. Hall

Making Words by Patricia M. Cunningham and Dorothy P. Hall

More Alternatives to Worksheets by Catherine Hiatt, Doug Wolven, Gwen Botka, and Jennifer Richmond

Teacher's Guide to Reading and Language Skills by Donna M. Miller

The Super Book of Phonics Poems by Linda B. Ross

"Best Practice"? Insights on Literacy Instruction from an Elementary Classroom by Margaret Taylor Stewart

Beyond Storybooks: Young Children and the Shared Book Experience by Judith Pollard Slaughter

Book Talk and Beyond: Children and Teachers Respond to Literature edited by Nancy L. Roser and Miriam G. Martinez

Celebrating Children's Choices: 25 Years of Children's Favorite Books by Arden DeVries Post, Marilyn Scott, Michelle Theberge

Developing Reading-Writing Connections: Strategies from the Reading Teacher edited by Timothy V. Rasinski et al.

From Literature to Literacy: Bridging Learning in the Library and the Primary Grade Classroom by Joy F. Moss and Marilyn F. Fenster

In the First Few Years: Reflections of a Beginning Teacher by Tina Humphrey

Journey of Discovery: Building a Classroom Community Through Diagnostic-Reflective Reading to, with, and by Children by Margaret E. Mooney

Talking Classrooms: Shaping Children's Learning Through Oral Language Instruction edited by Patricia G. Smith

Worm Painting and 44 More Hands-On Language Arts Activities for the Primary Grades by E. Jo Ann Belk and Richard A. Thompson

 **Answer Key**

Skills Assessment........page 6
1. str
2. ch
3. sk
4. br
5. sp
6. nk
7. sh
8. st
9. bowl
10. paw
11. light
12. cow
13. bread
14. book
15. sunset
16. fireworks
17. pinecone
18. lighthouse
19. doorway
20. unhappy
21. It's
22. coming
23. children
24. won't
25. books
26. boxes

Ride the Rails ....page 9
1. nut
2. rat
3. mug
4. tape
5. nose
6. rope
7. mop
8. nine
9. rug
10. top

Down the Slide ....page 10
1. cat (or cow, cookie)
2. desk (or dime)
3. leaf (or look)
4. sun (or seal, seven)
5. cow (or cat, cookie)
6. seal (or sun, seven)
7. look (or leaf)
8. dime (or desk)
9. cookie (or cat, cow)
10. seven (or sun, seal)

Bathtub Fun! ....page 11
1. f
2. v
3. p
4. b
5. f
6. p
7. b
8. v
9. b
10. f

Here's the Clue.........page 12
1. hat
2. hand
3. kite
4. well
5. wall
6. kid
7. hug
8. hill
9. ham
10. wave
11. kick
12. home

What Was the Queen Doing? ....page 13
The queen was "eating bread and honey." This rhyme is from "Sing a Song of Sixpence."

Our Earth...................page 14
1. t
2. d
3. t
4. d
5. t.
6. d
7. t
8. n
9. t
10. t
11. n
12. t

Rhyming Riddles.......page 15
1. less mess
2. hiss kiss
3. deep heap
4. lip zip
5. bug mug
6. pig wig
7. hop mop
8. pup cup
9. glass class

What's Missing?........page 17
1. e
2. a
3. o
4. a
5. e
6. e
7. a
8. o
9. a
10. o
11. o
12. a

My Dog and I...........page 18
1. beg
2. dug
3. tug
4. fed
5. mop
6. rug
7. red
8. lunch
9. hug
10. hot
11. bed
12. job

The Best Nest ....page 19

Across
1. win
4. ten
6. top
7. set
9. dog
10. rat
11. nip

Down
2. nut
3. mop
5. nest
6. tag
8. tan
9. dip

My Code ....page 21
Hi Joe,
I hope you can read this note. I wrote it in code. I will call you on the phone later.
I have a new joke to tell you. It is about a mole in a hole. I heard it from Mike. He came to my house on his new bike. It is very nice. He rode almost a mile to get here.
When I get my bike, you and I can ride to the park. We can take a hike. We can play hide and seek. We can go down the slide.
I will save my dimes to buy ice cream cones. We will have a fine time! Did you like my note? Please write back!
Your pal,
Ike

A Day Riddle ....page 23
1. with
2. cheer
3. much
4. other
5. this
6. ditch
7. than
8. they
Riddle: Thursday

Whale of a Word ......page 24
Riddle: alphabet

Scrambled! ....page 25
1. whale
2. ship
3. shells
4. chew
5. wheel
6. shoes
7. when
8. then
9. check
10. sheet

E or I? ....page 28

Like I:
sky
by
why
dry
fly
my
shy
try

Like E:
baby
very
city
any
many
story
copy
only

0-7424-2832-X *Reading for Every Child: Phonics*

Answer Key

Free Time ....page 29

1.	car	7.	bark
2.	park	8.	her
3.	far	9.	dark
4.	slippers	10.	star
5.	yard	11.	hard
6.	fern	12.	jar

Stirring the Soup ....page 30

1.	bird	7.	horn
2.	corn	8.	nurse
3.	curl	9.	shirt
4.	fork	10.	storm
5.	fur	11.	thorn
6.	skirt	12.	cord

A Sweet Treat ....page 31

1.	peak	7.	peas
2.	peel	8.	tree
3.	read	9.	cheek
4.	seed	10.	peach
5.	sheep	11.	queen
6.	feet	12.	seal

Beetlerella's Bug Ball ....page 35

1. glow show
2. low crow
3. boat coat
4. snow show
5. roach coach
6. Mole Bowl
7. toast roast
8. float coat
9. croak soak

Stack and Spell ....page 34

1.	st	7.	sc
2.	sc	8.	sp
3.	sp	9.	st
4.	st	10.	sp
5.	st	11.	sc
6.	sp	12.	st

Fish School...............page 35

1. black sack
2. blame game
3. bloom room
4. glad dad
5. cub club
6. rock clock
7. bass class
8. lap clap
9. purr blur

A Slippery Puzzle ......page 36

Across		Down	
1.	sleep	1.	slice
3.	flock	2.	planet
5.	float	3.	flame
6.	flat	4.	slip
7.	plus	5.	flute
8.	please	6.	flea
10.	sled	8.	plate
11.	plan	9.	slimy
12.	plane	10.	slow
13.	fly	11.	play

Crab Walk ....page 37

1.	dr	7.	dr
2.	br	8.	br
3.	cr	9.	dr
4.	dr	10.	fr
5.	fr	11.	cr
6.	br	12.	fr

Train Tracks ....page 38

1.	train	7.	proud
2.	track	8.	trade
3.	tree	9.	grin
4.	try	10.	grass
5.	press	11.	green
6.	price	12.	grow

One Night's Knots.....page 39

1. Kn, Knights
2. kn, knee
3. kn, knuckle
4. kn, knot
5. wr, wrist
6. kn, kneel
7. wr, wrap
8. wr, write
9. wr, wrote
10. kn, knows
11. kn, knock
12. wr, wrong

Spring Flowers ....page 40

1. spl, splash
2. spr, spray
3. str, strap
4. str, strange
5. spl, splinter
6. str, straw
7. spr, spring
8. str, street
9. spl, split
10. spr, sprout
11. str, string
12. str, strong

A Trip to the Bank.....page 41

1.	nt	7.	st
2.	nk	8.	nt
3.	nt	9.	st
4.	st	10.	st
5.	nt	11.	st
6.	nk	12.	nk

The Old Tower...........page 42

1. old
2. bald
3. lamp
4. cold (or damp)
5. damp (or cold)
6. myself
7. shelf
8. gold
9. stamp
10. told
11. child
12. bump

Down for the Count....................page 43

ou family:	ow family:
couch	brown
proud	frown
bounce	howl
house	down
shout	clown
pound	growl

Ship Ahoy! ....page 44

1.	coin	7.	foil
2.	boy	8.	noise
3.	voice	9.	joy
4.	choice	10.	point
5.	toy	11.	join
6.	soil	12.	boil

A Good Book......................45

1.	look	7.	took
2.	noon	8.	hood
3.	moon	9.	zoo
4.	wood	10.	goose
5.	room	11.	book
6.	foot	12.	tooth

Under took:	Under moon:
look	noon
wood	moon
foot	room
took	zoo
hood	goose
book	tooth

Compound Words ....page 48
1. bathtub
2. airplane
3. afternoon
4. downstairs
5. baseball
6. blueberry
7. butterfly
8. daylight
9. anyone
10. grandfather
11. homework
12. lighthouse

Everything, Except Onions ....page 49
1. anybody, anywhere, anyone, anything
2. everybody, everywhere, everyone, everything
3. somebody, somewhere, someone, something

Play Ball! ....page 50
1. basketball
2. baseball
3. football
4. kickball
5. fastball
6. handball
7. snowball
8. meatball
9. softball
10. volleyball

Rays of Sunshine ......page 51
sunrise
sunset
suntan
sundown
sunburn
sunroof
sunlight
sunbeam
sunscreen
sunblock

Compound Critters...page 52
1. goldfish
2. starfish
3. jellyfish
4. lionfish
5. blowfish
6. hummingbird
7. bluebird
8. blackbird
9. mockingbird

Compound Words Puzzle...................page 53
Across
1. snowflake
4. bedroom
5. pinecone
7. bobcat
9. sunset
10. butterfly

Down
2. airport
3. afternoon
6. jellyfish
7. baseball
10. homework

Feel the Beat ....page 55
1. 1
2. 2
3. 2
4. 3
5. 3
6. 1
7. 2
8. 2
9. 2
10. 3
11. 2
12. 3

Dividing Syllables.....page 56
1. cot/ton
2. sup/per
3. ar/row
4. al/low
5. com/mon
6. ham/mer
7. lad/der
8. ar/rive
9. tun/nel
10. nar/row
11. val/ley
12. wil/low

Chipmunk's Challenge ....page 57
1. al/mond
2. car/toon
4. chim/ney
6. thir/teen
8. mar/ket
9. gar/den
10. num/ber
11. cir/cus
12. mon/key
13. um/pire
14. wel/come
15. win/dow

Taking a Walk ....page 58
1. talks, talked, talking
2. waits, waited, waiting
3. plays, played, playing
4. laughs, laughed, laughing
5. whispers, whispered, whispering
6. works, worked, working
7. turns, turned, turning
8. prints, printed, printing
9. opens, opened, opening
10. cleans, cleaned, cleaning
11. stays, stayed, staying
12. wonders, wondered, wondering

Wolfs or Wolves? ......page 59
1. lunches
2. dishes
3. boxes
4. cities
5. pennies
6. wishes
7. benches
8. loaves
9. berries
10. leaves
11. wolves

Adding Endings ....page 60
1. clearer
2. kindest
3. colorless
4. hopeful
5. powerful
6. smaller
7. careless
8. neatest
9. quicker
10. wonderful

A Bushel of Apples ...page 61
1. girls
2. dogs
3. tables
4. chairs
5. rooms
6. desks
7. doors
8. books
9. pencils
10. rulers
11. markers
12. windows

One Sheep, Two Sheep ....page 62
1. leaves	7. men
2. wolves	8. sheep
3. children	9. mice
4. knives	10. feet
5. women	11. geese
6. deer	12. teeth

The Dog's Bone ....page 63
1. belongs to a boy
2. belongs to a girl
3. belongs to a dog
4. belongs to a cat
5. belongs to a pig
6. belongs to a bird
7. belongs to a frog
8. belongs to a cow
9. belongs to a knight
10. belongs to a friend
11. belongs to a mouse
12. belongs to a duck

Untidy Room ....page 64
Across	Down
1. untrue	2. unpaid
5. renew	3. unhappy
7. unable	4. reheat
8. relive	6. rerun
10. unmade	7. uncolored
11. retake	8. remake
12. repaint	9. rewrite
	10. untied

You're a Winner! ....page 65
1. aren't	7. weren't
2. isn't	8. won't
3. haven't	9. doesn't
4. hadn't	10. won't
5. wasn't	11. hasn't
6. shouldn't	12. aren't

I'll Call You Later ......page 66
1. She'll	9. She's
2. That's	10. They'll
3. There's	11. It's
4. He'll	12. We'll
5. He's	13. Here's
6. I'll	14. They'll
7. He's	15. I'll
8. We'll	16. What's

Two Peas in a Pod ....page 67
1. two	8. knew
2. too	9. two
3. to	10. to
4. too	11. no
5. no	12. know
6. know	13. new
7. new	14. knew

Dear Deer ....page 68
1. deer	8. dear
2. dear	9. meet
3. meet	10. meat
4. meat	11. beat
5. beet	12. beet
6. beat	13. meat
7. deer	14. meet

Missing Marks ....page 69
1. know, question mark
2. to, period
3. bear, exclamation mark
4. here, question mark
5. won, exclamation mark
6. be, period or exclamation mark
7. road, question mark
8. wood, period
9. one, period
10. rode, period
11. right, question mark
12. bee, exclamation mark

Fill-It-In Puzzle ....page 70

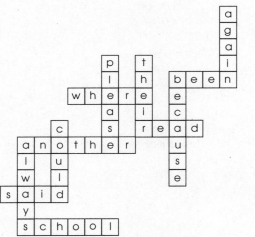

Morning ABCs ....page 71
1. always	7. have
2. been	8. found
3. have	9. morning
4. color	10. some
5. read	11. been
6. know	12. know

Eight on My Plate .....page 72
1. bright	8. gum
2. fry	9. good
3. kite	10. go
4. thigh	11. right
5. bite	12. pale
6. wood	13. night
7. need	14. eight

Friends to the End.....page 73
1. land	9. after
2. sleep	10. found
3. speak	11. last
4. small	12. near
5. shout	13. cry
6. raise	14. show
7. stack	15. more
8. fast	16. night

The Floating Hand ....page 74
1. *The Floating Hand*
2. Ima Riter
3. writes the words to the story
4. Drew Pichers
5. draws the pictures to go along with the story
6. fiction
7. five
8. "Bump in the Night"
9. 28
10. Answers will vary.